Trul

& Cheesy

Pirates

Facts & Jokes

Published in Great Britain in MMXIX by
Book House, an imprint of
The Salariya Book Company Ltd
25 Marlborough Place, Brighton BN1 1UB
www.salariya.com

ISBN: 978-1-912537-88-4

SALARIYA
SCRIBO BOOK HOUSE SCRIBBLERS

1 3 5 7 9 8 6 4 2

A CIP catalogue record for this book is available from the British Library.

Printed and bound in China.
Printed on paper from sustainable sources.

Created and designed by
David Salariya.

Author:
John Townsend worked as a secondary school teacher before becoming a full-time writer.
He specialises in illuminating and humorous information books for all ages.

Artist:
David Antram studied at Eastbourne College of Art and then worked in advertising for 15 years before becoming a full-time artist.
He has illustrated many children's non-fiction books.

Truly Foul & Cheesy™ Pirates Facts & Jokes

This Truly Foul & Cheesy book belongs to:

....

Written by John Townsend

Illustrated by David Antram

BOOK HOUSE
a SALARIYA imprint

Introduction

Warning – reading this book might not make you LOL (laugh out loud) but it could make you GOL (groan out loud), feel sick out loud or SEL (scream even louder). If you are reading this in a library by a SILENCE sign… get ready to be thrown out!

Disclaimer: the author really hasn't made anything up in this book (apart from some daft limericks and jokes). He checked out the foul facts as best he could and even double-checked the fouler bits to make sure – so please don't get too upset if you find out something different from someone wearing an earring and eyepatch shouting 'aarrrrrgh', anyone called Jolly Roger or a parrot with a wooden leg called Captain Flint (but who knows what its other leg is called?)

official warning

Don't be fooled by all those swashbuckling adventure stories where jolly pirates find chests of buried treasure and escape on spectacular sailing ships to beautiful tropical islands. The real world of pirates was brutal, cut-throat and deadly.

After all, pirates are no more than violent robbers on water. In fact, the word 'pirate' comes from the Latin 'pirata', which means sailor or sea robber, and from the Greek word 'peirates', meaning 'one who attacks ships'. There's nothing very glamorous about anyone who seizes or destroys ships at sea or in port. Pirates have done this for thousands of years, such as attacking the trading routes of ancient Greece, or robbing grain and olive oil from Roman ships. The Vikings were some of the fiercest pirates in Europe. They raided and looted between the 8th and 12th centuries.

Thousands of pirates around the world were terrorising sailors in the 1600s and 1700s – often called the 'Golden Age of Piracy'. After reading this book, you might call it the 'Gruesome Age of Gross'. You're about to discover how life on the high seas could be foul, disgusting and scary. There again, some of the cheesiness coming up may make you cringe. Brace yourself – you have been warned...

Loopy limerick

There was a young pirate named Molly
Whose parrot squawked
'I'm Pretty Polly',
Till she fell into ice
And froze in a trice...
Oh golly, now Polly's a lolly!
(What you might call a polygon.)

Riddle time

Q: What has 8 legs, 8 arms and 8 eyes?
A: 8 pirates.

Q: What do you call a pirate with two eyes, two hands and two legs?
A: A beginner.

Guess the saying

There's a pirate phrase that's quite well-known.
So can you guess this teaser?

It's when you take a plank of wood
And shove it in the freezer.*

*'Shiver me timbers' (In fact, this wasn't a real pirate saying at all, but a phrase made up by Robert Louis Stevenson in his famous pirate story *Treasure Island*.

What do you know about pirates?

3 myths to throw overboard from the start...

1 Pirates went around saying 'Arrrr', 'Mateys' and 'Me 'earties'.

Sorry – that's just made-up twaddle. Blame Hollywood for that myth. The 'pirate accent' as we know it today goes back to 1950 and Disney's film of *Treasure Island*. The actor Robert Newton played the pirate Long John Silver and he went a bit over-the-top with an English West Country accent. He did the same in *Blackbeard The Pirate*, and so the familiar pirate voice was copied by everyone. In fact, many pirates were Welsh, Scottish and Irish or even 'a bit posh', so just rememberrrrrr that on Talk Like a Pirate Day every 19th Septemberrrrr (yes, there really is such a day).

2

Pirates wore eyepatches, kept parrots as pets and had wooden legs.

Although a few pirates would have worn eyepatches, it's doubtful that many wore them. The idea that pirates wore eyepatches to help them keep one eye adjusted to the dark for seeing below deck is unlikely. Although there are some records of parrots being kept as pets on ships, very few pirates were likely to have one perched on their shoulders. Of course, many pirates would have had all kinds of injuries, including bad legs, but it's unlikely they would survive very long with a wooden leg and crutches on a ship.

3 The age of pirates disappeared a long time ago.

Sadly, pirates are still with us – mainly in the Pacific and Indian Oceans. Worldwide losses from piracy are thought to be 13 to 16 billion US dollars per year. Modern pirates, like those of centuries ago, steal ships and their cargo, as well as kidnapping, injuring and murdering their victims.

Foul alert

Missing limbs (look away now)

No doubt many a pirate lost an arm or a leg in fights, accidents or from infections, but their chances of surviving wouldn't be very high. A spot of swashbuckling could get your arm hacked off and getting shot by a musket might give you a bullet wound. Wounds soon became infected and could start to rot.

With no antiseptics or antibiotics in the 18th century, someone with a badly damaged limb had to have it removed before gangrene set in (when it turned black and 'died'). The only treatment was to chop off the limb. The way they went about it was to strap the injured person to a table, have a few men hold him down, give him a good shot of rum, and then put a strap of leather in his mouth to stop him from screaming. You can imagine the rest.

Once a leg stump was bandaged, the limping pirate hobbled off. Many still died after such an operation.

In *Treasure Island*, Robert Louis Stevenson gave Long John Silver a missing leg to make him memorable, while J.M. Barrie gave his pirate a hook hand and the name Captain Hook to make him extra scary in the story of *Peter Pan*.

Silly limerick

The arm of a pirate called Andy
Got crushed by a barrel of brandy
Then he noticed in books
How pirates wore hooks
So he cried 'Ooo arrrh, now that be so handy.'

Cheesy alert

Q: Why is pirating so addictive?
A: They say once ye lose yer first hand, ye get hooked!

Q: What's the difference between a pirate and a fruit farmer?
A: A pirate buries his treasure, but a fruit farmer treasures his berries.

Q: Why has no one ever taken a photograph of a pirate with a wooden leg?
A: Because a wooden leg can't take photographs.

Q: Where did Long John Silver buy his crutches and wooden leg?
A: Aaarrrrgos.

Did you hear about the pirate who bought his wife a wooden leg for Christmas? It wasn't her main present – just a stocking filler.

Just so you know...

There were different sorts of pirates. The privateers were 'official' as they gave some of their treasures to their country's king or queen. Buccaneers were privateers who 'hunted' in the Caribbean Sea during the 17th and 18th centuries. Corsairs were the same, but they sailed the southern shores of the Mediterranean Sea off North Africa.

Loopy limerick

On a pirate ship sailing from Libya
A fight lost the captain his tibia.
With leg wrapped in his shirt
He screamed, 'It don't hurt!'
But, of course, he was telling a fib-ia.

Buccaneers

Buccaneers invented a special kind of weapon called a cutlass, which was a short, heavy sword with a curved blade for slashing. In the 1650s, buccaneers had hideouts on Jamaica. Port Royal was known for its wild pirates and runaway slaves until it was destroyed by an earthquake in 1692. Corsairs also fought with curved swords, but they were called 'scimitars'. They were often used when kidnapping victims before selling them as slaves.

Cue for 3 terrible jokes...

Do you know how much it cost a pirate to buy two new earrings? A buck-an-ear (a buccaneer).

Did you hear about the corsair captain whose hearing was so sharp he could hear a pin drop in a howling storm during a gun fight? It must have been due to his many ears: a left ear, a right ear and a ship full of privateers.

They say that pirates are tough. So tough, that they never cry. But...that's not true. They do cry, but when they do, it's always behind closed doors – what you might call shedding a private tear.

Terror of the pirate flag

Just imagine your fear if you saw a ship heading your way with a skull and crossbones on its flag. You'd know you were about to be attacked, taken prisoner or killed. You'd also know that the Jolly Roger flag wasn't the sign for anything jolly. In fact, it isn't certain where that name came from. As ships once flew red flags to warn 'no mercy will be given', the name may have come from the French 'Joli Rouge' ('pretty red') – or maybe the term for the Devil, 'Old Roger', was to blame. Some pirates preferred to use their own personal design for a flag. As you might have guessed, the scarier the flag, the better.

Did you know?

Although Hollywood films might show pirate ships as dramatic galleons with three or more decks and masts with billowing sails, most pirates used smaller ships called galleys. These were long and narrow with banks of oars rather than sails. Unlike the sailing ships that they attacked, galleys could be rowed against the wind and in any direction. So pirates had to have strong arms for rowing – as well as for waving swords and pistols and dragging bodies!

Risk assessment

Not many pirates lived to a ripe old age. If they survived storms, shipwrecks, navy cannons or pirate squabbles, other dangers were always lurking. Foul food, disgusting drink and revolting diseases were never far away.

Foul alert

Pirates spent a lot of time eating dried biscuits and salted meat and swigging rum. They weren't known for their 'five-a-day' fruit and vegetables. After only a few months of not eating enough fruit with vitamin C, they could show signs of scurvy. That's bad news, and pirates knew all about it but not what caused it. They knew they had it when their teeth started falling out, their skin turned nasty, their legs got very fat and they bled from all over the place. They also had to keep dashing to the toilet (a bit tricky in the middle of a good swashbuckle).

Untreated scurvy was a killer and the only thing needed to recover from it was a suck on a lemon. It wasn't until 1795 that British sailors were given lime juice to prevent scurvy.
Sailing in the tropics could be risky. All those biting mosquitoes spread fever through many a pirate ship. Yellow Fever didn't make for a pleasant trip. Some pirates got better from it, but others just vomited black blood and died. Dirty drinking water or food infested with maggots or flies could give deadly dysentery, which is terrible stomach ache, swelling inside and death from diarrhoea. Do you still fancy the pirate life?

Famous British privateers

Because England and Spain were at war in the mid 1500s, Queen Elizabeth I encouraged English sailors to become privateers. John Hawkins and Francis Drake agreed to attack Spanish ships, then steal their treasures.

Sir John Hawkins (1532–1595) became a privateer and the first English slave trader. Along with his cousin, Sir Francis Drake (1540–1596), he took part in several expeditions to attack the Spanish, including the Spanish Armada in 1588. Despite his robbing of foreign ships, he and Drake were seen as heroes.

In 1595 Sir John Hawkins joined Drake on an expedition to attack Spanish ships in the West Indies. But even they weren't safe from the dreaded dysentery on board ship. John Hawkins died at sea off the coast of Puerto Rico. A few months later Drake died in Panama and was buried at sea, wearing his full suit of armour and in a lead coffin. It obviously sank without trace as divers have yet to find it.

Why the earrings?

Pirates wore earrings for all sorts of reasons. Apparently, some believed the rings would improve their eyesight or stop seasickness! They could certainly help their hearing when all those cannons were going off with a huge blast, followed by flying cannonballs. That's because some pirates would try to stop themselves going deaf by hanging wads of wax from their earrings for stuffing in their ears as earplugs around firing cannons.

Pirates feared dying at the bottom of the ocean (known as Davy Jones's Locker) or being washed ashore without the funds for a decent burial. So, their gold or silver earrings were also a form of insurance to make sure they could pay for a decent funeral and coffin. Some pirates engraved the name of their home port on the inside of the earrings so that their bodies could be sent home for a proper burial.

Many pirates even believed that a gold earring could prevent them from drowning, but that myth was disproved every time a pirate fell overboard and didn't appear again.

Q: Why are pirates' earrings so shiny?
A: They just ARRRR!

Q: What were the pirate's words when he blew out the candles on his 80th birthday cake?
A: Aye matey!

Q: What do you get when you cross a pirate's parrot and a shark?
A: A bird with an eyepatch that talks your head off.

For the record

Just in case you find yourself in a quiz, here's a little fact to keep up your sleeve (rather than a hook). In the famous pirate novel *Treasure Island* (written by Robert Louis Stevenson in 1882), the one-legged pirate Long John Silver had a parrot which cried 'pieces of eight'. The parrot's name was Captain Flint.

Pieces of eight were the world's first global currency. They were Spanish coins (each worth eight Spanish 'reales') and were used across much of the world when Spain had a huge empire. In 1600 one coin would have been worth the equivalent of a modern £50 note.

Cue for a joke

A pirate had tattoos scratched on his arm showing coins known as pieces of eight. The eight little tattoos in a circle turned itchy, then became very sore, so the pirate went to the doctor. After examining each tattoo, the doctor said: 'It's alright – they're benign.' The pirate replied: 'No, no doc, there not be nine, there only be eight.'

Daft limerick

In a lighthouse on rocks just off Brighton
Lived a pirate – all sailors he'd frighten.
Many ships ran aground,
And their crews often drowned...
As he'd not go to sleep with the light on.

Weapons

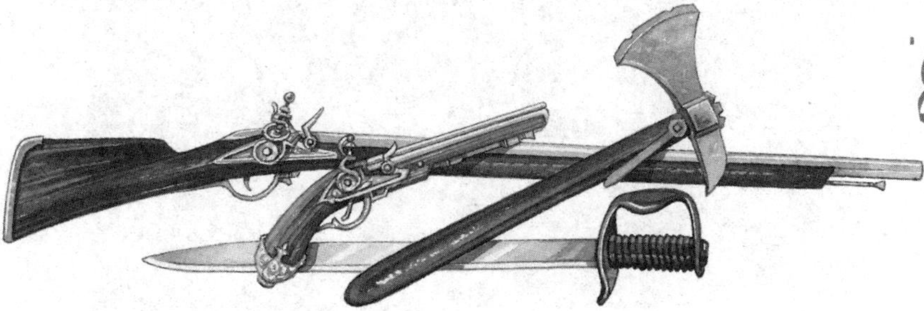

If you think the life of a pirate is for you, you'll need to know how to handle gunpowder. Apart from being a dab hand with knives, cutlasses and axes, you'll need to be a good shot (which wasn't so easy with early pistols).

Try these for size:

The Buccaneer Musket was a large and heavy gun, reaching almost 2 metres long. At first it was used for hunting wild animals on islands, but it was also handy for shooting someone on an enemy deck 300 metres away.

The flintlock pistol was much smaller and lighter – just right when boarding ships. Pirates often carried more than one as it needed reloading after each shot. Blackbeard had six with him at all times. How scary is that?

Blunderbusses fired shots all over the place. They were loaded with a handful of pistol balls and caused a lot of damage when fired over the deck. Not for the faint-hearted.

Grenades could be lethal when hurled onto a ship or thrown below decks. About the size of a cricket ball, a grenade had gunpowder inside, with a wooden fuse sealed with wax. After being lit, it took about 6 seconds to explode. Pirates would often throw these onboard an enemy ship just before boarding it, to cause serious damage and utter panic.

Now I've got this whip,
I feel like lashing out!

Warning

If all that shooting and swashbuckling seems exciting and you're **STILL** tempted to become a pirate… don't forget that pirate-hunters would be after you. They were paid big rewards for catching pirates and handing them over to be publicly punished as a warning to others. Look away now if you're squeamish…

Captured and convicted pirates were hanged in front of large crowds. They were often executed by hanging and placed on a gibbet built close to the low-water mark by the sea or a tidal section of a river. Their bodies would be left dangling until they had been submerged by the tide three times. You can imagine how crabs and lobsters would do their worst! If the bodies of notorious pirates needed to be preserved longer for public display, their corpses might be coated in tar. Sometimes, body-shaped iron cages were used to contain the decomposing corpses. There was nothing like a nice family day out to the beach to see a dead pirate or a pirate's head stuck on a pole as a jolly seaside display. Yuck.

Just for the record: in 1241, an Englishman called William Maurice was the first pirate known to be hanged, drawn and quartered. In other words, he was strung up, cut open for his insides to be pulled out, then his body chopped up. Not many pirates survived that!

A long walk off a short plank

If you still insist on becoming a pirate… watch out for other pirates. After all, pirates were in competition with each other for booty (valuable stolen goods). If an enemy pirate ship took you prisoner, you'd have to face torture to make you tell where you'd hidden any treasure.

So just get ready to walk the plank. Actually, pirates hardly ever made prisoners walk the plank (apart from in films). In case you need reminding, this punishment involved pirates forcing anyone they didn't like to be blindfolded, before walking across a plank hanging from the side of the ship. Plunging off into the swirling sea and shark-infested waters would soon finish you off. Although this fate was very rare, a report told of the fate of a crew of a Dutch ship captured by pirates in 1829. Apparently, the pirates fastened heavy shot and cannonballs to the victims' legs to ensure they'd sink – then forced each person to walk the plank one at a time.

Scary pirate tricks

Get ready for some of the more common punishments given out by grumpy pirates…

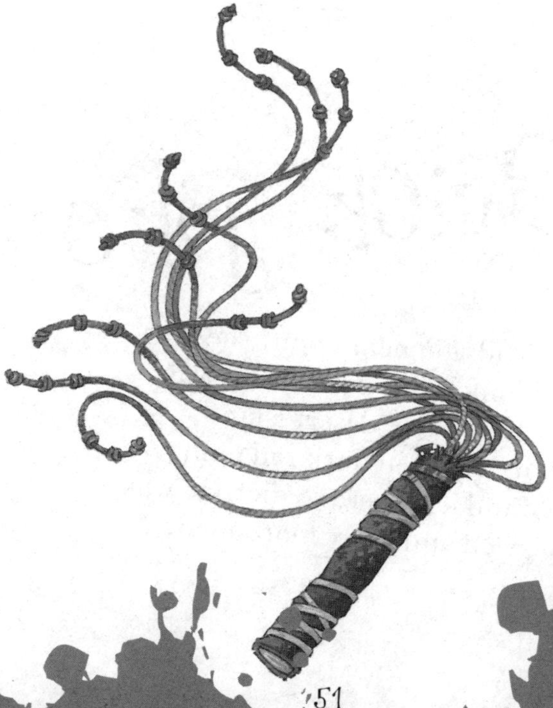

Marooning

This punishment awaited victims of pirate attacks or other pirates who did something wrong. The victim would be rowed to a remote island and dumped there, with little hope of surviving or being rescued. Sometimes a pistol was left on the island to allow the prisoner a quick death rather than starving or being attacked by wild animals.

Quick joke

Did you hear about the unpopular pirate who was taken to a desert island, covered in dark red paint and left there to die? He was well and truly marooned.

We want to buy you a present so we're having a whip round.

Slavery

Crew members who broke the rules onboard were likely to be sold as slaves. The money raised would be shared among the remaining pirates. And, of course, any pirate who disagreed could be dunked in the sea all day, being tied up and suspended from the Yard Arm.

I hate being a prisoner - it causes a chain reaction.

'Water, water everywhere and all the boards did shrink; water, water everywhere, nor any drop to drink.' I hate that poem.

Irons

Upset a pirate and you could be locked in wrist and leg irons called bilboes. These would fasten you to the ship's deck or in the rigging in all weathers. You'd probably die of thirst and heatstroke or shiver to death at night. It rarely ended well.

Tell me where the treasure's buried and I'll let you off the hook.

Torment

It might seem playful but this was a cruel entertainment at a victim's expense. The pirate crew would poke and prod a prisoner with cutlasses, swords and hooks. It was impossible to dodge all the blows as you'd be tied to a mast by a short rope. That meant a lot of hopping, ducking and 'dancing' around the mast while being accompanied by the ship's fiddle and plenty of teasing. Not for the emotionally vulnerable.

Keelhauling

Imagine having lead weights fastened round your legs and being tied to a rope hanging from the ship's yardarm. Then you'd be dropped overboard on one side of the ship, to be dragged right under it across the ship's keel and up on the other side. Apart from being slowly drowned, you'd be shredded by all those sharp barnacles on the ship's bottom. And there's nothing worse than barnacles on the bottom for an uncomfortable way to spend an afternoon. Ouch!

Burning

With all the barrels of gunpowder on pirate ships, it was easy to make a prisoner talk.

1 Pop the prisoner in a gunpowder barrel and threaten to light the fuse.

2 Tie up the prisoner with plenty of rope pushed between the fingers and toes and in the mouth. Then set fire to the rope.

3 If all else fails, barbecue the prisoner on a spit. They'll tell every secret they know.

Cheesy limerick

When Bluebeard was shot and harpooned,
He fell off his ship from his wound.
All his blood came to be
Why it's called the Red Sea
And his blue beard was promptly marooned.

Even cheesier joke

On a pirate ship out on the high seas, the First Mate was up in the crow's nest looking out for danger. Suddenly, a huge wave came from nowhere and slapped the side of the ship so hard it rocked violently to and fro. The First Mate fell from the crow's nest, smashing through the upper deck and crashing right down into the middle of the ship with a thud. The Captain peered down with his one eye and asked the First Mate if he was alright. 'Aye Captain,' he answered, 'I be fine. Arrrrfter all, I've been through many hard ships in my time.'

3 silly riddles

1 Q: What instrument did the pirate play in his band?
A: The guitarrrrrr.

2 Q: What do you call a stupid pirate?
A: The pillage idiot.

3 Q: Where does a pirate get a haircut?
A: The BAAAARBER at the HAAAARBOUR.

10 pirates you wouldn't want to meet at sea

(or anywhere else)

Riddle – who am I?

I was a famous pirate
Notorious and feared
My scary mass of facial hair
Gave me the name __________

Henry Morgan (1635–1688)

This lucky pirate was born in Wales and became one of the richest and most successful pirates ever. That's if you measure success by not getting caught, killed or badly injured. Considered handsome and dashing, he lived to the grand age of 53, which was good-going then, especially for a pirate. Not many enjoyed a wealthy retirement like him – as Governor of Jamaica, no less.

Morgan was a buccaneer because he set out to attack enemy ships and Spanish colonies in Central America. He and his crew sailed the Caribbean and robbed huge amounts of wealth – literally ship-loads of pieces of eight.

In 1669 Morgan led a fleet of eight ships and 650 sailors who ruthlessly attacked Spanish cities, killing anyone in their way. Next, he raided the city of Panama with a force of 30 ships and 1,200 buccaneers. After conquering the fort, his army hacked through the jungle towards Panama. Although exhausted, they defeated Spanish forces and raided the city, which was left in ruins, burned to the ground. Morgan and his men tortured and killed many to find where all the treasures were kept.

Now, you might expect the British King (Charles ll) to be pleased with Morgan for causing such trouble for the old enemy, Spain. Well, yes and no. The two countries were now supposed to be at peace, so English troops arrested Morgan and took him back to London. Was he punished as the ruthless pirate that he was? No. The king gave Morgan a pardon for all his 'good work' and gave him the very nice job of looking after sunny Jamaica. Nice work if you can get it.

Captain Kidd (1654–1701)

Some people think William Kidd was a ruthless pirate, others said he was no more than a privateer defending British ships from enemy attacks. Either way, he got into trouble for robbing on the high seas at a time when laws were changing to ban privateering. It didn't end well for him.

William Kidd was born in Scotland in 1654, the son of a Scottish Minister. While working as a privateer, Kidd gained a reputation for being brave. He soon became ship's captain, but his crew threatened to mutiny unless they could attack any ship around. So that's just what he did – stealing silk, gold, silver, sugar and rum worth a huge fortune.

After sailing to the island of Madagascar, several of Kidd's crew deserted him, so back he went to the Caribbean where he was now a wanted man. Before he was arrested and returned to England to go on trial, Kidd apparently hid much of his treasure – which many people have searched for ever since – everywhere between America and the Indian Ocean.

Captain Kidd was found guilty of piracy and taken to Execution Dock in London on the north bank of the River Thames – the final hanging place of many pirates. In 1701 he was strung up for all to see, with the rope around his neck suddenly breaking. He had to be strung up a second time in front of a jeering crowd. His corpse was put in a gibbet at the mouth of the Thames and left to rot, as an example to other wannabe pirates. The message was clear: piracy was not a good career choice.

Henry Avery (1659–?)

Avery was born in Plymouth, with some records spelling his name as 'Every'. He went to sea as a boy and served on several merchant vessels, as well as navy ships when England went to war with France in 1688. He then became a slave trader and pirate – a legend in his own lifetime. Some people saw him as something of a hero, believing he only attacked foreign ships and refused to attack English sailors (although he surely did).

Avery was admired by many pirates for his capture of one of the biggest prizes on the seas – the Grand Moghul of India's treasure ship *Ganj-i-Sawai*. It was packed with incredible treasures worth a fortune. But Avery and his closest crew didn't want to share the hoard with his pirates on other ships, so he played a trick. He loaded his own ship and arranged to divide it between everyone later. Instead, he took off at speed and the other ships couldn't catch up. Avery headed for the lawless Caribbean, where he bribed the governor of New Providence to protect him and his crew, even though King William III of England offered a reward of £500 for Avery's capture.

Some reports told of Avery sailing to Madagascar with his loot, where he set himself up as a king, with his own fleet and thousands of men. Other stories told of him returning to England – but no one knows when or how he died. It seems he was never killed or captured, and after just two years as a pirate captain, he'd escaped with more treasure than most pirates could even dream about.

Blackbeard (1680–1718)

One of the scariest of all pirates was Edward Teach (sometimes recorded as Edward Thatch), who was a big man with a bushy black beard. Known simply as Blackbeard, he preyed on ships in the Caribbean, around the coast of Mexico and along the east coast of North America.

Born in England (probably Bristol), Blackbeard joined an English pirate ship in 1716, before capturing a French ship that he renamed *Queen Anne's Revenge*. He became her captain. He fitted her with 40 big guns and his own flag showing a skeleton with an hourglass (meaning your time was about to run out) and a spear stabbing a heart. If that wasn't scary enough, big Blackbeard wore long boots, a wide-brimmed hat and slings full of pistols slung across his body. Before an attack, he would set light to slow burning fuses in his beard and long black hair. These fizzed with sparks and smoke, puffing out a cloud around him. Any sailor would be terrified and give up a fight before it started. He always threatened to kill anyone who put up a fight but he'd show mercy to anyone who surrendered peacefully. He led his gang of killer pirates for two years before the British Navy caught up with him off the coast of Virginia.

Lieutenant Maynard faced the fearsome Blackbeard who was shot five times and slashed about twenty times. The fight continued until Blackbeard staggered across the deck and fell. Maynard brought down his sword and cut off the pirate's head, to display on the bowsprit of the navy's ship. A legend tells that Blackbeard's headless body was thrown into the sea, where it swam around the ship three times before glugging below the waves to disappear forever. Treasure hunters have been searching for Blackbeard's hidden gold (if he actually hid any) and his headless skeleton on the seabed ever since.

John 'Calico Jack' Rackham (1682-1720)

John Rackham was an English pirate who became known as Calico Jack because of his clothes made from brightly-coloured Indian Calico cloth. He was the pirate who apparently came up with the design for the Jolly Roger flag of a skull with two crossed swords beneath it.

Most of Rackham's pirate raids were in the Caribbean, with plenty of plundering, swashbuckling and merrymaking in seaside bars. That was until the British Navy finally caught up with him. At the age of 37, he was arrested and went on trial in Jamaica. Calico Jack and his crew were convicted of piracy and sentenced to hang. Like so many others, he was taken to Gallows Point in Port Royal and publicly executed. His body was later taken down to be displayed in chains, swinging from a gibbet – his calico pecked by the birds.

Bartholomew 'Black Bart' Roberts (1682–1722)

This famous Welsh pirate captured and looted more ships than all the other famous pirates put together. That was more than 400 ships in four years. His 'success' was down to his skill and daring, even though he didn't set out to be a pirate. Roberts was an officer on board the slave ship *Princess* in 1719 when he was captured by pirates under Welshman Howell Davis.

For someone who didn't want to be a pirate, he turned out to be good at it and was given the job of captain when Davis was killed.

Roberts and his men sailed to Newfoundland and found 22 ships in the harbour. Everyone there fled at the sight of his black flag, so Roberts and his men looted and sank the ships. Later that year (1720), the pirates captured other ships, so Roberts now led a fleet of pirate gun-ships. Scary!

Next it was off to the Caribbean, where Black Bart and his crews captured dozens of ships. Roberts now owned a fortune but he was killed in action by pirate hunters off the coast of Africa in 1722. This is a description of him as he fought his last battle:

'Roberts himself made a gallant figure, being dressed in a rich crimson damask waistcoat and breeches, a red feather in his hat, a gold chain round his neck, with a diamond cross hanging from it, a sword in his hand, and two pair of pistols hanging at the end of a silk sling.' ('There's posh', as they'd say back in Wales.)

Suddenly, a cannon shot tore out his throat. His men threw his body overboard and surrendered. 152 pirates were arrested and swiftly put on trial. Many were hanged.

Olivier Levasseur (1690ish–1730)

This French pirate was nicknamed La Buse ('The Buzzard') because of his speed in swooping on his enemies in ruthless attacks. He was born in Calais to a wealthy family, was sent to a good school and soon became a respectable naval officer. He realised he could make big money by raiding Spanish ships and working as a privateer for the French King, Louis XIV. A story tells of him getting hurt in a sword fight, leaving a scar across one eye. He then wore an eyepatch over it, so maybe we have him to thank for the popular image of pirates in eyepatches.

In 1730, Levasseur was finally captured for his violent attacks at sea and sent to the island of Réunion off Madagascar in the Indian Ocean. It was here where he was hanged for piracy. According to a legend, as Levasseur was standing on the scaffold with the noose round his neck, he managed to throw a coded message into the crowd, telling them that his treasure would belong to the person who managed to work out his secret code. So far, no one has been able to crack the code and find the treasure – which could well be worth over a billion pounds.

Maybe it said this: My treasure is buried in the **DDDWDDDEDDDSDDDTDDD** (**'WEST'** in Ds = West Indies. Get it?) Alas, his message was far more complicated.

Anne Bonny (1697–1782)

Anne Cormac was born in Ireland and married a sailor called John Bonny. She then left him for what she thought was a more exciting life with Calico Jack Rackham. The world of pirates wasn't just for men, she insisted. Even so, whenever she fought, she dressed as a man and killed anyone who suspected she was a woman. She fought fiercely and proved she was as tough as any man.

Anne and Jack patrolled the Caribbean, looting ships and gaining a reputation as ruthless buccaneers. The crew included Mary Read, who became Anne's close friend. That was until their ship was captured in 1720 by pirate hunters. Most of her crew hid below deck while she and Mary fought to defend themselves. They were soon taken prisoner, along with Captain Jack Rackham who was hanged for piracy. Anne and Mary couldn't be executed as they claimed to be pregnant. Anne was kept in prison until she gave birth. What happened next was never recorded but possibly her father paid for her release and she may have started a new life. Some reports said Anne Bonny died at the grand age of 82, but no one really knows for sure what happened to her in later life.

Mary Read (1695ish–1721)

Born in England, Mary Read was brought up by her single mother, who dressed Mary as a boy (as her dead half-brother) to make sure they still received maintenance money from his grandmother (yes, it's a bit complicated). This male disguise continued when Mary needed to get a job at the age of 13. Eventually she joined the British military and went to sea. When on a ship sailing for the West Indies, she was taken prisoner by English pirates. Because she was dressed as a man, they allowed her to join their crew. Mary continued to dress as a man, because all sailors and pirates believed women on their ship brought bad luck. Within a few years, Mary joined a pirate crew captained by John 'Calico Jack' Rackham. Her disguise meant no one suspected she was a woman – not even fellow pirate Anne Bonny at first.

How do I keep so fit?
Ooh aaaah, gym, lad!

Mary got into all sorts of scrapes, including fights with other pirates, whom she would kill with a sword or pistol – apart from the one who fell in love with her. But her fighting skills didn't stop her being captured in 1720. Pirate hunters stormed her ship, with Mary and Anne left to defend it while the rest of the crew hid below deck. Mary fired her pistol in the hold and screamed at them to fight like men. They were all arrested and put on trial in nearby Jamaica, where many of the crew were hanged. Mary was also found guilty of piracy but her execution had to wait for her to have her baby in a few months' time. However, she caught a fever and died in prison at the age of 31.

My husband was a human cannonball until he got fired.
Mine too but he was useless - not the right calibre for the job.

Limerick time

There was a young pirate from Bristol
With a taste for fine gold and cut crystal.
He would rob and be ruthless,
Was heartless and toothless,
Till he met Mary Read with her pistol.

Ching Shih (1775–1844)

In a ten-year span, Ching's 'Red Flag Fleet' (about 400 Chinese twenty-gun junks and several thousand pirates), sailed up and down the coast of China, robbing ships, towns and anywhere with something to plunder.

The dreaded Red Flag Fleet of pirates was ruled with ruthless cunning by Captain Ching Shih, with her determination to be the most feared pirate in history. She and her pirates caused terror along the Chinese coastline. She would sometimes take her shallow-bottomed boats and row them up small rivers to attack towns that were unguarded.

In 1808 the Chinese government organised a navy to set sail and attack the Red Flag Fleet. You might have thought that was a good time for Ching to lie low for a while. Wrong. Ching couldn't resist a fight. She sailed out to meet the navy head-on. In the battle, she captured 63 ships from the Chinese Navy. The captured sailors had a choice: either join her pirates or be tied down to the deck and beaten to death with clubs. Hmmm – tough choice.

Ching was tough and insisted on a code of honour from her men. Rules were strict. Any of her pirates who stole from her would be beheaded. If any tried to leave her fleet, their ears were cut off. No one messed with Ching. For some of her men, her name brought a shiver of fear, for others it brought the sound of riches… what you might call ker-**CHING!** Her wealth continued to grow with every raid.

In 1810, Ching accepted an offer from the Chinese government. If she and her force of thousands of men and hundreds of ships sailed into port for the last time, they would be allowed to keep all their stolen hoards and not be punished. Ching agreed and chose to retire, and she lived to an old age with her riches and fearsome reputation intact.

Pirate timeline

700 BC Reports of pirates around ancient Greece.

100 BC Reports of pirates around ancient Rome.

200 AD Piracy increases in Asia after the fall of the Chinese Han dynasty.

700–1000

Vikings from northern Europe make raids along coastal areas in North America, Europe and North Africa, and along inland routes by river.

1300s

Rise in piracy around the Mediterranean. English and French fleets combine forces in battles against African-based corsairs.

1400

Klaus Störtebeker, one of the most famous German pirates, is beheaded.

1500s

Rise in ocean trade traffic brings a big rise in piracy. Ships and towns are attacked in the newly-discovered America.

1557

Conflict between England and Spain sees the rise of privateers, such as Sir Francis Drake.

1623–1638

The Caribbean becomes a haven for pirates. Over 500 ships are destroyed or raided in 15 years.

1650–1680

Britain and France attack Spanish shipping lanes and ports, beginning the 'Golden Age of Piracy'.

1690s

Caribbean-based pirates sail to the Indian and Red seas in search of trade ships sailing to and from India. Pirate Captain Henry Avery captures an Indian treasure ship full of riches – one of the biggest pirate hoards.

1701

The trial and execution of famous Scottish pirate, William Kidd.

1718

Blackbeard is killed in battle.

1720

Captain Jack Rackham and his two female shipmates, Anne Bonny and Mary Read, are captured. Rackham is hanged.

1722

The wealthiest pirate of his time, Welshman Bartholomew Roberts, is killed in battle.

1716–1730

The final stage of the 'Golden Age of Piracy'. Many ex-privateers refuse to stop robbing ships when European countries are at peace. The navies of Europe and America seek them out.

1775–1800

Piracy returns to the Atlantic and Mediterranean during the American Revolution and Napoleonic Wars.

1807

Female pirate captain Ching Shih (also known as Zheng Yi Sao) leads thousands of Asian pirates in the China Sea. They retire in three years.

1820

Policing of oceans halts piracy around Central America.

1850

Piracy is under control in Asian waters.

2000s

A rise in pirate activity around Somalia on the East African coast.

And finally...

From cheesy jokes to the super-sophisticated(ish):

- Did you know that apple pies cost $3.00 in Jamaica and £4.50 in Barbados?

So much for pie rates of the Caribbean.

• By the way… To err is human. To arr is pirate.

• Did you know 3.14% of sailors are Pi-rates?

Final joke

A pirate captain found a crumpled old map showing where treasure was buried. He was determined to find the chest of gold and silver, even though the map showed it was buried in a deep swamp in the middle of an island. His pirate crew had doubts. The swamp was known for swallowing people up and drowning them. Only two of the captain's men agreed to go with him to dig up the treasure. After dropping anchor near to the island, the captain and his two men rowed ashore before hiking to the edge of the bubbling swamp.

'Ooo arrrr, it looks mighty dangerous,' one of the pirates gasped. 'It be dead risky,' said the other. 'Ye be right cowards,' the captain snapped, as he took off his boots and waded into the swamp. His companions expected to see him sink up to his neck or disappear under the festering bog. Instead, the swamp only came up to just below his knees, so he sloshed his way through before screaming. 'Aaaah, I've cracked my shins on something hard. I reckon it be the treasure chest.'

The others laughed. 'It would be buried far deeper than that.' Sure enough, the captain reached down and dragged up a chest. 'Here 'tis. This be it – in just half a metre of water. So it's true what they say… **BOOTY IS ONLY SHIN DEEP!'**

Final limerick

On his death-bed, a pirate called Trevor,
Wrote a limerick that's ever so clever.
He went into decline,
As he wrote the last line,
So...

???

If you survived some of the truly foul facts and cheesy jokes in this book, look at the other wacky titles in this revolting series. They're all guaranteed to make you groan and squirm like never before. Share them with your friends **AT YOUR OWN RISK!**

QUIZ

1. What was a Jolly Roger?

a) A very happy pirate

b) A famous pirate's parrot

c) A pirate flag

2. What was a disease that some pirates suffered?

a) Parrotitis

b) Scurvy

c) Woodworm

3. Who was the pirate in Treasure Island?

a) Long John Silver

b) Short Jack Bronze

c) Wide Jim Gold

4. What was a blunderbuss?

a) A passenger ship

b) A weapon

c) A pirate swearword

5. What was keelhauling?

a) A type of pirate dancing

b) A type of pirate punishment

c) A type of pirate cooking

6. Who was Edward Teach?

a) Bluebeard

b) Blackbeard

c) Bloodbeard

7. Who was a famous female pirate in the 18th century?

a) Bonny Clyde

b) Bonny-Ann Read

c) Anne Bonny

8. When was the Golden Age of Piracy?

a) Roman times

b) 1650–1720

c) 1830 till midnight

9. Which of these pirates was NOT Welsh?

a) William Kidd

b) Bartholomew Roberts

c) Henry Morgan

10. How was the German pirate Klaus Störtebeker executed?

a) Tickled to death

b) Beheaded

c) Fed to sharks

Answers:

1= c
2= b
3= a
4= b
5= b
6= b
7= c
8= b
9= a
10= b

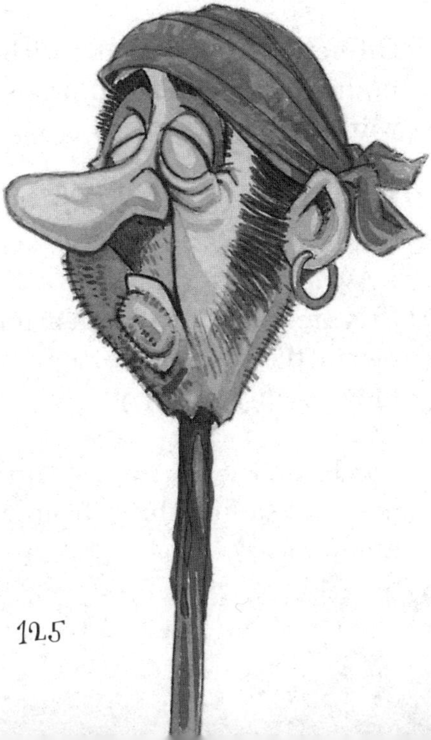

GLOSSARY

Bilboes: iron bars with sliding shackles, used for holding a prisoner's ankles.

Buccaneer: sailors who attacked enemy ships in the Caribbean Sea during the 17th and 18th centuries.

Corsair: privateers operating along the southern shore of the Mediterranean in the 16th–18th centuries.

Cutlass: a short sword with a slightly curved blade, once used by sailors .

Gibbet: an upright post with an arm on which the bodies of executed criminals were left hanging as a warning to others.

Musket: a muzzle-loading gun with a long barrel, fired from the shoulder.

Privateer: a sailor on an armed private ship permitted by its government to make war on ships of an enemy country.

Yardarm: the horizontal timbers mounted on the masts of sailing ships, from which the square sails are hung.

INDEX

I finished reading this Truly Foul & Cheesy book on:

........../........../..........